The Problem Solving Kata as a Tool for Culture Change: Building True Lean Organizations

Mohammed Hamed Ahmed Soliman

Published by personal-lean.org, 2022.

Table of Contents

... 1
Introduction ... 4
Recruiting the Right Habits ... 5
Embedding Improvement into the Day ... 10
When Psychology Gets in the Way ... 12
Classroom vs. Continuous Coaching ... 16
Developing Your People Improves the Process ... 19
Distinction between Lean Leadership and Classic Management Approach ... 21
Leadership Development Stages ... 25
Turning PDCA into a Learning Cycle ... 31
Lean Culture to Support Financial Department ... 37
Improving Accounting Process, the Flow of Information, and Financial Documentation ... 38
Appendix I ... 48
Process Improvement and Value Stream Mapping ... 50
References ... 53
About the Author ... 57

Dedication

I created this book with the help of more than fifteen different business resources. These academic articles and books are all cited at the end of this book. A number of people have influenced my learning journey and my entire career. I would like to acknowledge them here.

Esraa Soliman: My lovely wife and partner. She encouraged me to write and publish this work. In fact, she always encourages me to do creative work.

Jeffrey Liker: Professor at the University of Michigan and author of *The Toyota Way* and the amazing Toyota series of books. His impressive work on Toyota inspired and influenced my learning about the Toyota Production System. I would really like to thank him for his indirect involvement in this work. Many examples included in this book were originally from his books. Although I have never met Jeff face to face, we have had great communications over social media platforms.

Chris Duklet: A lean manufacturing leader from the United States who works in the field of health care. He has contributed to this work by reviewing the book prior to publication and giving me useful recommendations and advice.

Attia Gomaa: Professor at the American University in Cairo who influenced my teaching career at the university and taught me how to become a good trainer.

Steven Borris: A business consultant, author, and friend from England who influenced my writing career. He encouraged me to write and publish. Steven was my mentor on lean manufacturing, helping me first to understand the basics, after which I developed my understanding through deep practice and self-directed learning.

Eslam Soliman: My friend and a professor at the Assiut University. His PhD is from the University of New Mexico. He has influenced my entire writing career by giving me recommendations and advice on how to write and publish. He revised my published works many times and kept inspiring me after every piece I wrote and published.

The Problem Solving Kata as a Tool for Culture Change
Building True Lean Organizations

Copyright ©2022 Mohammed Soliman
All rights reserved

While every precaution has been taken in the preparation of this book, the publisher assumes no responsibility for errors or omissions, or for damages resulting from the use of the information contained herein.

CULTURE CHANGE THROUGH PROBLEM SOLVING KATA: BUILDING TRUE LEAN ORGANIZATIONS

First edition. November, 2022.

Copyright © 2020 Mohammed Hamed Ahmed Soliman.

Written by Mohammed Hamed Ahmed Soliman.

Introduction

Some businesses have reduced staff and made resource cuts to survive the global economic downturn, while others have improved business practices and culture. Unfortunately, there is still a difference between successful and less successful businesses in terms of culture adaptability, people management, and process management. In organizations like Toyota, which, in contrast to its rivals, has a mindset of process improvement, culture drives competitive advantage. Other businesses might benefit from Toyota's teachings by changing their routines for behaving and thinking in order to increase staff performance.

In his book *Toyota Kata*, Mike Rother wrote that none outside of the Toyota group of companies has successfully brought systematic continuous improvement into all processes every day and across the organization. Even Toyota's efforts to spread its approach of continuous improvement to outside suppliers have not met expectations.

Truly, most organizations remain far away from establishing a solid continuous improvement system, and current management behavior rarely leads corporations to do what they should do in terms of both process and people management. Bad habits, behaviors done with little or no conscious thought, continue to affect culture and hold companies back from success.

Recruiting the Right Habits

One of the initial steps for business success is getting the right people on the board with the appropriate skills and attitudes. How companies choose and hire their people reflect their organizational culture. These hires are going to develop new methods of working, invent new products, lead the transformation and build a successful business. They are the company's future leaders.

But do companies really get what they expect from their hiring candidates?

Traditionally, companies demand degrees and certifications to demonstrate expertise, while others prefer to hire based on experience, history and skills. Neither way will work if the organization in question refuses to develop a culture of improvement. Managers hire MBAs and Six Sigma black belts with the mistaken notion that they will transform the business without a transformation of management.

Yet what can a certificate holder do in a system that doesn't engage employees in the continuous improvement cycle, value their ideas and develop them continuously? A closer look at these companies reveals that they don't have a real system capable of utilizing and aligning employee skills and efforts to solve problems and achieve business goals. Your entire professional force can get certified, but if the company culture doesn't allow it, they won't get the chance to practice what they have learned.

And while certificates can prove ability, actual improvement will not occur without a high commitment to self-education and self-development to keep the certificate holder's knowledge up to date, allowing the person to develop better ways of working and practicing. Certificates don't drive performance competency in the practical world.

Josh Kaufman, author of international best-seller *Personal MBA*, wrote that a large body of evidence suggests that what some business schools teach has no connection to what is required for business success. Unfortunately, according to Kaufman, many business programs have de-emphasized value creation and operations in favor of finance and quantitative analysis.

This extreme focus on financial analysis produces executives who are not capable of improving business performance, driving success and creating value for customers. It doesn't build distinguished leadership.

Reinforced by their MBA education, many executives and managers seek solid financial outcomes, although in many instances they have lost connection with the reality that exists on their organization's front lines. Decision-makers are poorly informed about the actual situation, and decision-making is based on incorrect assumptions and inappropriate targets. They have learned to manage the process via distance using some reported metrics. They have not been taught the culture of improvement.

For example, if managers remain behind the scenes and avoid actual place where the work is done (the gemba), they will not realize what small issues pop up as obstacles to success. They will make poor decisions. Then, when their business processes fail, the human resources department asks what went wrong. After all, they have hired professional qualified persons.

But hiring professionals won't, by itself, turn around an organization. However, having a real continuous improvement system and an embedded culture of improvement will. A system that empowers employees to make changes, motivates them in the right way, aligns goals and efforts with organizational strategies and vision, develops leaders continuously, bases management decisions on real situations, and makes improvement a part of everyone's daily routine is a system with a high chance of success.

Better questions, better results

When organizations base their hiring processes on certifications and classic interviews, what do the companies really know about these individuals, their behaviors and their openness to change? Do companies really get the results they need?

The hiring process can be improved to select better candidates if the human resources department, instead of asking for certifications, tests individuals properly and assesses their skills.

Toyota thinks approaches the hiring process differently. The powerhouse Japanese automaker wants to hire people who are motivated and highly committed to self-development and self-education. For Toyota to exceed customer expectations, its employees must do the same. Toyota tends to assess what its candidates know and how they are going to use that knowledge.

Jeffrey K. Liker's *The Toyota Way to Lean Leadership* originally reported that when Toyota started to hire leaders for the New United Motor Manufacturing Inc. (NUMMI) plant, the first joint venture plant between Toyota and General Motors, the focus was on hiring candidates who had demonstrated an inherent capacity for self-development and learning. Toyota wanted people who had an openness and excitement to learning new things.

Toyota also uses a system to test individuals for their abilities to work in a team. A group of candidates is placed in a meeting room and assigned a problem to solve. Toyota likes to hire the candidates who demonstrate the ability to function well in a team and devise a solution by working with others.

Organizations should use behavior-based tests and real assessments as part of any recruitment strategy. And this is where the application of industrial and organization psychology comes in.

In the book *Social Psychology and Human Nature*, authors Roy F. Baumeister and Brad J. Bushman reported that most companies use informal and unstructured behavioral interview questions like the following:

- What are your weaknesses?
- Why should we hire you?
- Why do you want to work here?
- What are your goals?
- Why are you leaving your job?
- When were you most satisfied in your job?
- What can you do for us that other candidate can't?
- What are three positive things your last boss can say about you?
- What salary are you seeking?

According to many psychologists and researchers, such traditional questions don't serve a company's real needs. Improving the hiring process to help generate a culture of change would involve using relative, reasonable and structured behavior questions such as these:

- Tell me in specific detail about a time when you had to deal with a difficult customer.
- Give me an example of a time when you had to make a decision without a supervisor present.
- Give me a specific example when you demonstrated an initiative in an employment setting.
- Give me an example of a time when you had to work in a team.
- Describe a time when you had to be creative at solving a problem.

Such questions tend to assess leadership and problem-solving skills, which is what most companies really need anyway.

Embedding Improvement into the Day

Often, employees don't focus on improvement because of the lack of "north goals" and the improper alignment of departmental goals with the organization's strategies and vision.

In the Toyota vision, "north goals" refer to the long-term vision, such as being the best automotive maker in the world or holding more than 50 percent of the market share. In his book Toyota Kata Mike Rother calls the process of setting targets and striving toward them in Toyota the "improvement kata," and management focuses each day on coaching employees on how to reach those targets – targets that are aligned with the company's long-term vision.

A kata is a series of practice moves to build on form and technique. For our leaders, we want them to be able to do two things: Systematically improve processes toward a clear target (improvement kata) and coach others on the improvement kata (coaching kata).

Improvement kata really describes the Toyota habits for continuous improvement. Toyota uses its improvement kata to make a way of a managing and working that we normally reserve for crisis situations. And the more often employees practice these new improvement behaviors, the more likely it will become a routine.

Concrete, stretch goals, aligned with organizational strategies, are the key to making improvement a priority. Stretch goals break down strategic goals into easy-to-understand bites that workers can digest and are a main way to cascade organizational values down from above to the front lines. For example, it means nothing to tell your employees that the goal is to be the leading supplier in the industry. But breaking that aim down into stretch goals yields metrics, such as "50 percent reduction in defects per year," or "20 percent productivity gains each year," that can measure results.

By repeating the continuous improvement cycle and using "smaller" stretch goals, organizations can achieve their long-term vision. Departmental goals should be aligned with the company's strategic objectives or the employees will wonder why they are bothering to improve the system. People tend to make progress on things they believe in. It is a part of any motivation program.

People should believe in the power of the system and that they are working to make their job and life easier and safer. The company's success is their success. This is where the intrinsic motivation comes from. If goals are not specified, people won't improve because they will think everything is fine.

But if the company has clear strategic goals, goals that are broken down into achievable metrics, employees will generate ideas and explain how their ideas are aligned with these goals. The system itself will drive the motivation and creativity of everyone. There will be no more need for financial motives that undermine performance and kill motivation. A system that trains supervisors and engineers to listen to the workers' problems and allows information can be exceptionally motivational.

When Psychology Gets in the Way

Think of your vision in business terms – such as No. 1 market share, zero warranty cost and 100 percent accountability. Break those down into stretch goals for your employees and departments to use. Make sure these stretch goals are concrete and aligned with your strategic business objectives by aligning them with the value you provide to your customers.

Goals can't be things like standardizing the work process, which simply opens up the work force's psychology to a host of questions. The human mind always seems to latch on to criticism of change. Workers will wonder why they are standardizing the work. After all, they're OK with the current process. Why should we put forth energy and effort instead of focusing on a higher priority? If improvement doesn't have a clear direction and assigned priority, people will consider it low priority and continue with their current methods.

As explained in Toyota Kata, Toyota inserted continuous improvement into its employee DNA by using the kata approach. Improvement became a part of each employee's daily routine, something that can't be achieved through formal trainings or classrooms.

Take, for example, the question "What do you want to do to improve your work?" The answer can be "We need to reduce setup times, apply a production pull system, remove wastes from the shop floor, reduce production lead-times and standardize work procedures." This is what most companies do, and it represents a poor alignment of goals with strategies.

Lean improvement, on the other hand, strives toward an objective. A better question would be "What is your target?" The answer could be "Meeting the customer demand rate (takt time)." This begs the question of what do the workers need to reach this target, which yields the answer that they need to improve the cycle time of their machines to meet the customer takt time.

The second case clearly defines customer takt time as a stretch goal to strive for. We know where we want to be. And improving machine cycle is a target condition that we must meet to reach our goal. It should be a measurable thing, like a cycle time of 50 seconds faster than the takt time. The first example has no target, and we could spin our wheels improving things while not knowing where we want to be or where this improvement will lead us.

One of the most fundamental mistakes made by many companies is trying to improve something without a clear strategy that serves the customer requirements and finally the success of the business. Definitely, meeting the customer demand rate will allow the organization to deliver products on time and achieve 100% customer satisfaction. This can serve the long-term strategic objective of being a leading supplier.

People and core values

You will need a strategy statement that articulates your vision and incorporates the stretch goals that are required to achieve it. Even if your people don't fully understand where you are taking them, repeating the words of your strategy will help them understand that they are part of a team going in the same direction.

These statements should be generic enough that your vision will fit any future acquisitions. It is important that your strategy defines the operational excellence that you envision. For example, be the leading supplier in your industry or be one of the globe's top 10 corporations.

Core values must be articulated. Achieving excellence requires teamwork, trust and respect for people. Core values are like guideposts that will point your workforce toward your ultimate goal of working in a culture of improvement.

The three main core values to consider are people, customer and quality. Respect for people is one of the Toyota production system's pillars and is the main reason for Toyota's success.

A policy of not laying off employees because of improving efficiency is a good thing to follow. Letting workers go after they improve a process will disrupt the whole system, and it means no improvement in the next time. Employee will resist change as long as it threatens their livelihoods. If a strategy of respect for people is set, then a 20 percent cost reduction target clearly means process improvement, not cutting resources. Always remember that a company can't change its core values every few years without losing the respect and confidence of its people.

Respect for people includes developing your leaders instead of outsourcing solutions. Many companies hire external experts. They create a continuous improvement department, hire the improvement consultants and relegate the improvement behavior to them. Such a parallel team will be powerless to effect change and make improvement. They don't know the company's culture or processes.

But when the outsourcing consultant leaves, all knowledge is gone. The regular employees have no experience to keep managing the improved processes or continuously improving them to face the future challenges. They have not been trained on the culture of continuous improvement and have not contributed to the transformation process.

Instead, lean tools should be used by the company's leaders and the factory managers who have the capability, power and responsibility to effect changes. Improvement should be done by people who are managing the work day by day, not by a parallel team. The leaders who manage work each day will be responsible for coaching people who do the work. And those people must own, operate, develop and continually improve their processes. Companies that travel the consultant route should make sure they use the temporary personnel to share lean expertise and knowledge with the rest of the workforce.

Classroom vs. Continuous Coaching

We learn by doing, and problems give us lessons to learn. What we learn through formal educational programs can't be standardized for all industries and cultures. What might work in one place won't work in another. Situations differ, even in the same industry. Anyway, classroom training, while it can only provide a specific level of awareness, does not change behaviors and culture.

Toyota uses a completely different pattern of learning. Toyota teaches its workers to develop solutions, not just to solve problems. The automaker's employees learn a routine of thinking and acting that harnesses the human capability to improve.

Many companies aim to teach their employees skills, delegating the process to the training department or human resources. Those departments might assess what employees know, their performance, and train them accordingly.

Instead, as a commitment to self-education and continuous development, Toyota's kata system continuously develops people and ensures that each mentee has a mentor. For example, the team member is coached by the team leader, and the team leader is coached by the group leader. This is Toyota's method for passing its improvement kata on to all organization members.

Continuous coaching at the workplace builds strong leaders. Embedding this into the organization's daily routine will make improvement a habit of everyone. This is a main reason why continuous improvement becomes a behavior pattern for everyone in Toyota's organizations. The learning cycles that Toyota leaders have to take, the continuous coaching at the workplace, and the utilization of problems as an opportunity to learn and grow have made Toyota a remarkable company.

As Liker explained in *Toyota Under Fire*, this is what allowed Toyota to come out stronger after several recall crises in the 200s. It helped Toyota stand out during the global recession.

Toyota doesn't rely on certifications and formal education programs. In fact, Japanese business culture doesn't think much of such certifications and MBAs because management and leadership should be taught at the gemba, where the actual work is done. This is where Toyota and many other Japanese businesses conduct most of their training.

Toyota's kata system is one of the best strategies ever created to learn and develop leaders. As Rother presented in *Toyota Kata*, Toyota specifies, aligns, and achieves the outcome targets via the improvement kata behavior. This process removes obstacles and keeps repeating the plan-do-check-act (PDCA) cycle at every step. At the same time, Toyota's coaching kata coaches' people on how to achieve their goals and meet target conditions. Toyota is teaching people across organization a behavior routine that aligns people and functions in accordance with the organization's philosophy and vision.

So how about you?

Start with a vision. For struggling businesses, a long-term vision of five or 10 years won't mean much if the company ceases to exist in 12 months. In this case, targets should be adapted to match the real situation to help the company survive.

Goals can be broken down into more manageable pieces and smaller increments. This ensures quality implementation. You also can apply the PDCA cycle slowly at every step and remove obstacles as they are found. It is preferable not to apply a large improvement at once. The obstacles and resistance to such change would be huge, and the entire program could fail quickly.

For each target, specify the current condition and the target condition using the appropriate metric. In many conditions, setting and trying to follow a long-term plan for making improvements is like moving in a road full of fog. Breaking the goals into smaller, stretch targets make them easier to manage, motivating your workers to strive for success. Specify a plan for reaching each target, make it actionable and give it a time frame. Get your people involved in how to do it, and listen to their ideas carefully.

It is important not to neglect the training. Most companies that fail to reach their improvement goals have neglected the training and coaching, which are necessary parts of the process. Managers should dig deep in the details to discover root causes rather than jumping to solutions and the "do" phase in the continuous improvement cycle.

Changing cultures and breaking old habits is the key to better performance. Cultural behaviors drive competency, company growth and continual success. Organization's culture need change if they want to embed continuous improvement into everyone's daily routine.

It is easy to talk and hard to do. It requires long-term management support and internal investment. Practicing new behaviors will shift the employees out of the existing routine and, over time, influence people's thoughts and actions. In the long term, repeated new habits can lead to a culture of continuous improvement.

Developing Your People Improves the Process

Throughout the years, lean leaders have become experts at improving processes. But in most cases, that's only a half-step. True lean leadership involves coaching and training your people so the improved process doesn't slip back from the ideal state, and the plan-do-check-act cycle is a remarkable tool for teaching.

The Toyota Way is held up by two main pillars: Continuous improvement and respect for people. And the good industrial manager knows that respect for people, which is about coaching, developing, supporting and valuing the workforce, is the foundation of continuous improvement.

Actually, people are more important than the process, and companies that put process before people will not earn sustainable results. People are the ones who build, operate, modify and improve the process. Therefore, developing people should be your company's highest priority. Focusing only on the process often will lead to system failure.

Early on, Taiichi Ohno, co-developer of the Toyota Production System, refused to document or write the system down for fear that people would focus narrowly on the tools and the theories. When he finally wrote it down, it was presented as a house because a house is a system. If you take away any of the structures that hold up the roof, the roof and entire system will collapse. One of Ohno's students said Toyota made a mistake calling it the Toyota Production System. Instead, Toyota should have called it the Thinking Production System because the real point was to make people think, and people are the value of the system.

Distinction between Lean Leadership and Classic Management Approach

Unfortunately, while many companies say that they value their people, they actually focus more on the process when using methodologies such as lean or Six Sigma. To develop a culture of improvement, you have to continuously coach and develop your people to change their habits, making improvement a routine.

In a classic management environment, managers who don't get results put pressure on their employees and push improvements. They are seeking quick results and short-term financial gain, not the long-term viable health of the organization. In bureaucratic management, managers take targets from the top and cascade them down to their workers, continually evaluating people using metrics. The ones who get the results are rewarded. The ones who fail might be punished.

Such leaders often are working to a financial plan, with the only care being climbing ladders rapidly and getting results at any cost. This is a classic example of managing people. And such leaders are separated from the reality of work because they don't take gemba walks to figure out what is really happening on the front lines.

On the other hand, the lean leader takes the target, breaks it down into manageable pieces and goes to the gemba to train, develop, improve and apply the method. This leader works horizontally to align the effort, method and plan across different functional departments with the company's business goal. This leader is seeking sustainable results. He works with people to solve problems. He goes to the gemba to learn deeply, develop himself and help others to learn and see. This leader is seeking the right process to get the right results by developing people through process improvement.

In the bureaucratic management system, people tend to hide their problems for fear of being blamed. This creates a dysfunctional culture unlike lean, which encourages problems to surface so they can be solved. Unfortunately, bad management habits will develop a negative culture that will continue to prevent organizational success.

Toyota uses improvement kata to develop a routine that will systematic continuous improvement into all processes. And Toyota uses the coaching kata to coach people on the continuous improvement process so they are capable of meeting the targets and facing the challenge. The early stages of the improvement kata should be practiced under the watching eye of the mentor. So, what makes good leaders?

Management by Objectives	Industrial Management using Hoshin Kanri for Direction Planning and Deployment
Invented by Peter Drucker 1954	Originated in Japan in 1961 and used successfully by Toyota and top-tier companies in US and Japan
Management based on command and control	Management is based on empowering, motivating, and developing people on problems solving skills
Focus on the results	Focus on the process not the results this include the plan, the method, the innovation, and people development & training on problems solving
Recognize individuals	Rewarding system is based on teamwork, overall performance and accomplishments
Promote individualism	Promote teamwork
Top-down method	Top-down with linkage to shop floor
Managing process via distance and rely on reported metrics	Managing on shop floor (gemba principle) and base management decisions on facts
Use metrics to evaluate people and results	Give people degree of autonomy and use metrics to monitor the work progress and understand the obstacles need to be removed to improve the process.

| Focus on the strategic thinking only | Link the strategic thinking to shop floor, use gemba as a management principle, and use visualization, standardization to improve the work |

Leadership Development Stages

Summarized by Liker in Toyota Way to Lean Leadership:

1. Committing to self-development

Toyota hires people who are committed to self-development and openness to change. You simply can't force people to learn if they don't want to. You can force them to take notes and give feedback, but psychological experiments have proved that such learning will remain at a superficial level.

If only a few people in your system know how to solve problems, one of them leaving will disrupt the whole system. So, your organizational target should be that everyone must learn and act. A company is strong because of its people, not its processes. And you have to standardize the learning process so it becomes a routine.

While people who are doing the work should be trained to improve the process, the real change always come from the top. For example, examine the New United Motor Manufacturing Inc.'s NUMMI plant, the first joint venture between General Motors and Toyota General. The initial aim of the Japanese was to train plant manager Gary L. Convis. Convis was in the most critical position. Training him was the key to then training everybody in the hierarchy. Then training could move down to team leaders.

While teaching comes from the top to bottom, a company's decision-makers are the ones who can transform the organization. So ideally, they would learn first. Of course, depending upon where you are in your corporate hierarchy, it could be difficult to persuade top management to visit the gemba regularly and get involved directly in the system's continuous improvement. If that's the case, training can start with the middle managers, supervisors and workers, who can select a small project to improve. Hopefully, early successes will convince top management of the importance of continuous improvement methodologies.

2. Learning to lead at the gemba

Few leaders go the gemba regularly. Some visit only when there is a problem. Others practice daily walks to observe people. To be a truly great leader, you have to learn how to lead at the gemba.

Gemba is the place where the value creating work happens. The real value from these visits comes from observing the actual situation at the processes, providing the needed support for the working teams, realizing what the actual situation is, making decisions based on facts instead of reported metrics, finding the root causes of the problems, improving the process, coaching people and improving people's safety and morale. Every lean tool that creates value and eliminates waste, from work standardization to value stream mapping, should be planned, applied, improved, adapted and standardized at the gemba. Gemba walks should be one of the main core values for any company that wants to develop good lean leaders.

When Toyota hires new managers or leaders, they are expected to spend enough time at the gemba to understand the process and gain the trust of the people. In other companies, the spent at the gemba varies.

For example, when Convis was asked to leave the NUMMI plant and become president of Toyota's Kentucky plant (he was the first American to become president of that plant), Toyota told him that he would first have to learn the culture, get involved in the work and get his hands dirty to prove he could handle becoming president. He was to go to the gemba to learn the jobs, understand the people and understand Toyota. Convis had a year to accomplish this. In most corporate cultures outside of the Toyota group of companies, it is unusual for a president to spend so much time at the gemba.

Japanese culture believes in what they call t-leadership, where you should become an expert in a particular technical area before moving to the next level. You have to know what people are doing before you can lead them. When you become expert in something, you can start learning the basics of other things but you may not go to have the same depth of knowledge in the other fields and you are going to relay on other experts in these fields.

As Jeffrey K. Liker, author of *The Toyota Way to Lean Leadership*, explained, Toyota develops t-leaders by moving those with high potential first up the chain of command in their specialty. Then such leaders can move horizontally to different specialties. This also teaches leaders to manage vertically and horizontally. Leading horizontally across organizations is important when trying to solve large problems that cross different functional departments.

In far too many industrial organizations, CEOs have no idea about the many different operations that include the supply chain, production, quality and the culture of improvement. How do you expect to manage an organization when you don't understand the processes? Such managers cannot solve problems across different functional departments if they have never been at the gemba in those departments.

3. Learning by teaching and developing others

Companies are made of people, and people are not perfect. So continuously developing leaders is the key for perfection, which should be an ultimate goal. When Toyota develops a leader, that leader is expected to become a teacher and develop another leader. It is fundamentally a coaching cycle and a one-to-one coaching method.

For leaders to become coaches, they must be able to assess the trainee skills objectively and find the gap between the skills the trainee has and the skills the trainee needs. Discover the trainee's strengths and weaknesses and then begin coaching. Avoid giving detailed instructions or pointing out the solution. Instead, as Mike Rother presented in *Toyota Kata*, ask questions to observe how the mentee is thinking.

Leadership development is a practical, problem-solving process. Any classroom time should be short, brief and only for the purpose of providing an awareness level. Classrooms don't lead to culture change, but training leaders at the gemba will. Mentees will only learn by doing, and they must practice on a real project. The sha hi ri model of learning detailed below is a good starting routine.

The leader must build trust with the student. If you aren't trusted as a mentor and coach, I won't follow your lessons. In Japan, as Liker explained in *Developing Lean Leaders at All Levels*, the master rarely praises the student. However, this culture didn't work very well with Americans in the Toyota plants. Therefore, Liker wrote, the Japanese conclude that every criticism should include three things that are positive.

The lesson here is that you can't coach everyone and every culture the same way. Your coaching model must adapt. But the principles are always the same. Critical feedback can be important because without it, mentees won't know what to learn to improve for the next time. Yet a cascade of positive comments might lead the trainees to think that they are the best and need to learn nothing.

Shu ha ri is a model of learning that comes from the martial arts presented by Liker and Convis in his *The Toyota Way to Lean Leadership*.

Shu means to protect, and in this phase, students are being coached on the fundamentals under the eye of the master. Students must embrace the routine and copy exactly what the master is telling them. There is no deviation accepted.

Ha means to break away, and in this phase, after the student has learned these routines and the basics have become natural, the student has more freedom to practice unsupervised and diverge from these rules. The master may check on the student, who can apply the rules creatively but still must follow the standard rigidly.

Ri means freedom, and in this phase, rules and behaviors have become so ingrained that the student no longer thinks about them consciously. Students then are in the position to develop their own understanding. The student is working beyond the rules.

Think about the work standard. A worker has to learn how to assemble parts onsite following the standard work procedures strictly. The student will learn by doing. In the shu stage, the student will see how the work is done and try to follow the teacher. The worker will practice the job continuously until he or she reaches the second step, ha. The teacher will keep monitoring the student until he or she reaches the final stage, ri. At that point, the worker can observe the overall working procedures and take the responsibility to improve it.

Turning PDCA into a Learning Cycle

Mistakenly, many people think plan-do-check-act (PDCA) is a continuous improvement cycle, even if they neglect the human part. PDCA does aim to improve the process, but if you have only improved the process without developing and teaching your people, you have put the process at risk of slipping back.

People must be trained in the culture of continuous improvement so they can keep managing the process with the new method. PDCA is actually a remarkable learning cycle because people learn by doing. The best thing is to pick up a real project and start improving a process. You don't learn to play football by watching a game or golf by watching the coach. You have to practice under the watchful eye of the mentor to develop new habits and change the bad ones. An attentive coach is critical to helping you make a new method become routine.

Toyota has several steps in its problem-solving process, steps that cycle through the famous PDCA wheel.

1. Define the problem relative to the ideal (plan).
2. Grasp the current situation.
3. Break down the problem into manageable pieces (plan).
4. Find the root cause of the problem (plan).
5. Develop countermeasures (plan).
6. Implement the solution (do).
7. Examine what the actual outcomes are (check).
8. Adapt, adjust, standardize and scale the solutions to other areas (act).

Note that the plan phase is invoked five times before proceeding to the do phase. This is to ensure both the quality of the implementation and that the selected countermeasure will solve the problem. Lean emphasizes the plan. And the plan phase cannot be created without a daily observation at the gemba to find the root causes, gather facts, discuss things with the process operators and develop the best countermeasure from different alternatives.

Unfortunately, many leaders jump into the do phase without spending enough time observing the situation to find the real problem. The most enjoyable part for the leader is the "do," but jumping to the do usually results in a quick fix that not only might not solve the real problem, it could create wastes in other linked areas.

Jumping to the do phase can escalate the problem. Take the example of electrical problems in automobiles. In this case, the technician decided that the problem was in the spark plug coils pack. Changing that costs $350 dollar. Unfortunately, that wasn't the problem – a faulty engine control unit (ECU) was. Replacing the ECU cost $1,500. The waste in time, effort and resources led to a total cost of $1,850.

Define the problem relative to the ideal to find the current and ideal states. You might consider your quality ratio of 97 percent good, but any gap between the current state and what could be reached is an opportunity for your competitors. One of the main failures in this step is how people hide their problems because they fear blame. There is no culture of visualizing problems and surfacing issues. This always makes it difficult to define the problem and discover the gap between the current state and the ideal state.

Grasping the current situation is critical. Management decisions should be based on facts, not simply metrics or computerized reports. This is why it's so important for managers to go the gemba to see what reality is. Watch the process and look to solve the problem, and remember not to blame the people.

Break down the problem into manageable pieces. We have seen many companies set targets and cascade them down to the bottom levels. The leaders below are responsible for achieving this target in a timely manner. Top management may blame leaders if this target has not been achieved on time. Upper management also often sets too big of a target, such as an 80 percent improvement in quality improvement this year instead of 20 percent improvement for four years.

This is another example of poor management habits. Psychological experiments have proved that people tend to make progress on concrete, small goals rather than complex, large ones. Seeking large improvements at once will cause a system failure, especially when people are new to process improvement. Leaders have to be patient. Breaking down the target into small increments will encourage people to participate and act.

When searching for the root cause of the problem, remember that at first glance the problem can appear to be a person. But leaders have to dig deeper to find the true root cause. Overconfidence is one of the biggest barriers to problem-solving. Leaders think they know how to fix things and will follow the problem-solving process at a superficial level. Without the true root case, you probably will build a plan and invest in resources for something that is not going to work.

Select the suitable solution from different countermeasures that you have received from people involved in the process and from different perspectives. Lean encourages selecting a solution from different alternatives. Prioritize your options and select the countermeasure that has the highest chance of success. Perhaps you can choose one that is easier to try and relatively inexpensive. Then you have to develop your plan on who, when and where.

However, it is possible that spending time in the plan phase will not reveal the proper solution. At this point, a small pilot project might be necessary in an attempt to reveal the appropriate countermeasures.

Only then can you go to the "do" phase and implement the countermeasures. Be careful, as many managers think that this phase is the end of the issue, and once they pushed the button the system will go live and run forever. Keeping the process monitored is necessary. Continue coaching and supporting people to avoid slipping back.

You should also use metrics and post them in the workplace. This helps align people to common targets. Those metrics should be visualized in the workplace using visual boards. Later, the progress should be updated and discussed regularly. Use colors for in-progress targets and for the achieved targets. The metrics give a starting point to your workforce. What is our measurable target? Where are we? Where do we want to be?

In the "check" phase, remember that after implementing the solution, people will not always continue in the same way as you wished. They won't follow the standard all the time. Supporting people, continuously motioning them, coaching them and developing them until the new way becomes a routine is the key to a perfect solution. You may not achieve this in the first PDCA cycle. So, you have to repeat it continuously and keep supporting people until the new standardized process becomes a routine.

The "act" phase is where the start of the next cycle begins. You next plan will be based on the feedback you received from the "check" stage. In this phase you, should figure out what did work, what didn't and standardize what worked.

Why develops people?

After the Toyota recall crisis several years ago, company President Akio Toyoda was quoted as saying that the corporation's rate of growth was higher its rate of people development.

The key success of Toyota's continuous improvement process is the effort that managers or leaders put in people development through the PDCA cycle. It is a remarkable learning cycle. As you go through each PDCA, you will learn different and higher levels of skills. This should be done under the eye of the mentor. Practicing new behaviors will shift the employees out of their existing routine and, over time, influence people's thoughts and actions. In the long term, repeated new habits can lead to a culture of continuous improvement. People should follow plan-do-check-act so often that it becomes natural way of thinking.

If a problem crops up that you thought had been solved, the proper question would be have you rotated the PDCA wheels enough times? PDCA needs to spin a lot before you reach your target, achieve a stable process and form new habits.

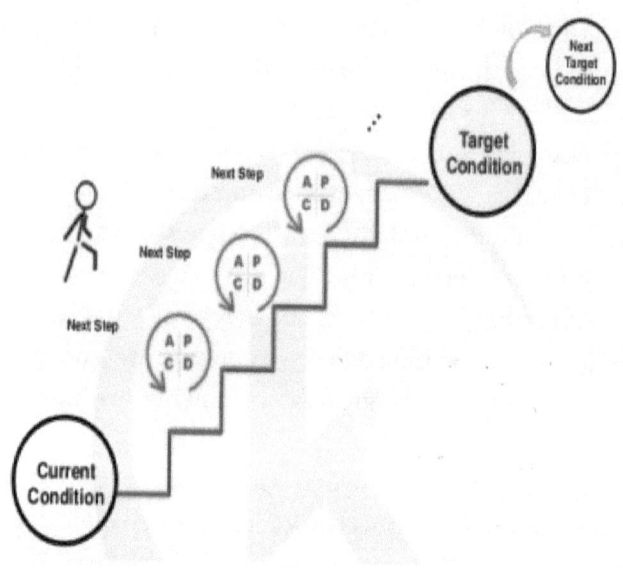

Lean Culture to Support Financial Department

Improving Accounting Process, the Flow of Information, and Financial Documentation

Making financial information more relatable to teams and departments within a company is the aim of applying the Lean concepts to accounting. Lean can be applied to accounting to eliminate this gap between the accounting domain and the rest of the company operations.

For the past decades, financial folks relied on old principles, techniques and theories in determining the performance of the companies and give feed backs to the executives and CEOs so they can make the necessary improvement and take decisions. The CEO wants help finding the resources to fund a new project; he wants to know where we can improve costs in products and services, and he wants to know whether improvements made have resulted in financial gain. The CEO needs help seeing where the company has improved or declined and what the future looks like given the current circumstances.

Unfortunately, many corporate management accounting systems are inadequate for today's environment. They haven't been improved substantially since then. A famous example of this is the use of ABC (Activity Based Cost) system. *Jean E. Cunningham and Orest J. Fiume* indicated that many companies have found ABC encourages batch processing in order to spread costs over a larger number of units in favor of reducing the unit/cost.

In the unique book *Real Numbers by Jean E. Cunningham and Orest J. Fiume,* the authors presented how for decades US was the world's manufacturing giant, home of quality and efficiency. Many industrialists didn't notice until too late that they were getting clobbered in the marketplace. Especially in the automotive industry, giants like GM, Ford, and Chrysler were losing significant market share to Japanese companies, led by Toyota.

Because most of accounting systems were mostly developed in the early 1900s to support manufacturing products in batches, these same systems now send wrong, and sometimes disastrous signals in a lean environment. It is like an island in the stream, the accounting areas have remained rooted to the methods that have been taught in business schools for decades.

If you work in an accounting department, look at where your department is and where people go during the day. Do accountants come in, sit at their desk and remain fixed there all day long? Are they far from the rest of the action? Do they ever go to the site where parts are being purchased, where products are being designed? If they do not, if people from through the business have to come to accounting to seek information, it is a good indication that the accounting team is sidelined!

Current financial models

Companies that are moving rapidly to lean and seeking to continuously improve their processes will find that the current financial model is not working because most of financial models are based on large batches which is against lean production. Lean is based on making to order (Soliman, 2015).

A classic example is the use of EOQ & EPQ formulas

The terms Economic Order Quantity & Economic Production Quantity have been around for many years much longer than lean methodology and Just in Time. EOQ was first developed by F. W. Harris in 1915. The problem is that EOQ is an old term from the old days getting used in a new world in a new way. It doesn't take into account many of the hidden losses. The major problem with EOQ is that the model is viewed as static. Using Lean, the model changes with every improvement.

Unfortunately, EOQ is still being taught in many international businesses, financial, and cost management programs in the universities and in all over the world without considering the dramatic change made by lean and the transformation to the material movement methods. *Making Materials Flow by LEI* provide the necessary material calculations for the lean environment (Harris, 2003).

The most common problems that can be found in the current industrial accounting & cost accounting processes that need to be adequate are summarized here:

1. Financial thinking is still stuck on batch production

One clear example for this is keeping a piece of equipment running constantly utilized because accountant said this machine must run constantly to make it profitable and keep unit cost low. So, company's buy materials it doesn't need, pay an operator to run parts that are not needed and puts unnecessary tear and wear on the machine. This is all done because accounting blessed the machine's purchase based on specific parameters, which included sales projections which were too optimistic (Ahmed, 2014).

In lean, if you don't need the parts, don't run the machine. The cost of resources spends to make unsellable products plus the cost of holding the inventory is greatly bigger than the cost of not utilizing the machines to their maximum capacity (Ahmed, 2014; Soliman, 2017).

2. Financial data arrives late and often misleading

When accountant deliver old news, what do we do with old news? Accountant in many instances spend a lot of time counting things and producing outdated reports while many of these costs can be easily expected and placed before the end of the month. If you want the information to be valued, don't give it to the executives after the activity is completed! In some cases, information is weeks late. In lean environment, immediate visual feedback is required in order to eliminate root causes and prevent problems from recurring to gain highly competitive advantage with your business operations.

3. Matching

All costs to manufacturer the goods you sell must be recognized as an expense in the month you recognize the revenue. Most costs need to be recognized in the month they happen. A practical example: the materials that you bought for a product that will ship in two months will be kept as inventory on your balance sheet. It is not an expense until you ship the product. The cost of advertising that product, or any other, is recorded as an expense on the books in the month it happens. This has been the genesis of a lot of standard cost accounting techniques. In lean, as lead time shrinks, products that are being made should be shipped in the same month so there is an opportunity to simplify accounting procedures and produce meaningful reports.

4. Moving rapidly to automation

In many companies I have seen, switching to automation became a source of cost reduction. In many instances, this can be just a form of transferring the costs from one area to another (from Direct to Overhead). Moving to automation without eliminating wastes is just like automating the wastes.

Taking the example of complex and expensive machines/lines that can combine several processes in one process, usually the cycle time of those machine slower than the cycle time of the other simple machines (cycle time is the time required to process one unit of product). Often those complex machines are not flexible in responding to the high increase in demand so you have to buy more expensive machines to expand your capacity if the demand was to increase.

At the other hand, if demand is decreased you are stuck with non-utilized expensive machines and this involve a high depreciation cost that you will have to pay independent of the production volume.

With the simple machines, they tend to cycle faster and usually perform fewer types of tasks/processes or only one process. They are better anyway in term of demand fluctuation. They can respond to demand increase or decrease more efficient and at lower costs.

Accountant also spend a lot of time trying to collect costs using bar codes and other modern methods. Without improving the process, itself, using advanced technologies can became another source of money wasting.

5. Financial statements

When financial statements became difficult to understand they became not trustfully, because we don't trust what we don't understand. The reports must be presented in a manner that can be read and easily understood by non-accountants.

Unfortunately, some business programs have gone the route of teaching all people in a business how to understand the numbers. Companies create classes for their employees to help them understand the numbers. Would not it be easier to make the numbers understandable? Non-understandable reports, inefficient reports and late reports can be all classified as waste.

6. Performance reports

All companies attempt to establish metrics to determine if they are achieving their goals. Unfortunately, many of these measures are too complex for average worker to be actionable, and some create dysfunctional behavior.

Also, there are many performance measures that you don't need or don't present the real state of the company. There are many other helpful measures that are available in the lean books and references which can be used to help executives make decisions.

Example, one of the business premier measures, stressed in most financial management programs and treated as one prevailing metric, is return on investment ROI, As currently practiced, ROI is an excellent example of the intent to capture many complex and interrelated events, thus creating one monster of a metric that few people can relate to their daily activities. ROI involve huge parameters and factors and should not be used as a standalone measurement and should not be used as the only measurement around. If everything is being counted in term of immediate or direct financial benefits, the indirect improvements to quality, down times and setups may not get the attention and the resources they deserve because everything is being evaluated in terms of financial benefit. Many direct financial metrics are not efficient in the modern environments and you have to develop your own ones and shift people's thinking so they can think more proactively in terms of company's success and customer. Liker (2003) quoted *"Base Your Management Decisions on a Long-Term Philosophy, even at the Expense of Short-Term Financial Goals."*

7. Stuck with cost accounting rather than cost management

It is far less important to count the cost of making a product that it is to manage the cost of the whole business. Traditional cost accountant is dependent on establishing a standard method for calculating the cost of making every product and every component the company make. In most of companies, the accountant department is trying to figure out the best method of calculating costs rather than trying to manage, reduce and plan the cost of designing and making this product.

Most studies show that 80-95% of the life-cycle cost of a product is committed during the design process. That mean only 15-5% of the total cost is susceptible to future cost reduction effort without redesigning the product.

8. Budget planning

Every year we see financial guys negotiating for a tough budget and operations guys negotiating for an easy budget so they can look good. In the end, the financial guys own the budget. Operations can say "It is not my fault you gave me a bad budget" Often this creates a lot of conflicts between operations and accounting. Financial guys always wait until the end to provide an evaluation and judge the situation, then report what went wrong. Would not be better for them to begin with the planning process and offer help? *Chief Financial Officer, Greg Flint quoted "I don't think budgets are worth a hill of beans. They are based on guess work and politics."*

9. Accounting process and non-value adding activities

Many accountants spend time doing non-value-added activities, record unnecessary information, produce unneeded data and duplicate things. Even the value-added work they do may arrive late (the reports) so it became obsolete and outdated. There is no systematic method to produce on time reports to help track the root causes of issues. What have gone wrong have gone wrong, what is the purpose from keep recording it??!

I personally found many accounting systems contain waste. As with any other business process, accounting processes can be improved to eliminate waste and allow for timelier reporting of valuable information (lean accounting).

What should we do?

Sometimes improvement has been blocked due to barriers created by accounting. If managers didn't notice the effect of improvement on the company's performance, they won't support the idea or commit to the resources required. How many times have we heard executives say, "What you really do has no benefit to the organization? I don't know what you are doing, but whatever it is, stop it, you are killing profits."

Involve your account people in the change. If they are not involved in change, they will remain mired in the old culture, along with batch processing and standard cost accounting. Accountants are not just a report generator, they are business partners.

Accountants should switch themselves from focusing on transaction processing or bean counting to becoming valued business partners who contribute meaningful information for decision-making purposes.

The goal of accounting education

The goal of an accounting education is not to prepare for a life time recording debits and credits, but to learn a language and tools to assist a business toward better performance.

As you continuously improve your process and make serious progress in the transition to lean manufacturing, you have to continuously improve the accounting method, keep accountant folks updated, educate them and get them involved in every step you make. This is to avoid the serious disconnect that will occur between the operations and accounting (Byrne, 2012).

What happened to cost management certification programs?

I personally hold a certification in cost management that is internationally accredited. And I'm pretty confident to say that it only served as start so you can begin thinking on how to improve the way things are being done in your organization. It didn't provide information on how lean accounting work or how to improve costs, just a background on how basically cost is being counted and planned so you can brainstorm where the defects are coming from. I got the knowledge through practicing lean and reading a lot of lean and continuous improvement references.

Appendix I

Process Improvement and Value Stream Mapping

There is no reason companies should not try to get rapid results with the overall implementation of lean. However, this should be done without neglecting the learning. Culture adaptiveness and leader development are very important in order to get sustainable results. Otherwise, the improvement will be short-lived. All efforts, resources, and tools spent to achieve the results will be lost.

Lots of companies tend to focus on improving as many individual processes as possible. They use tools such as value stream mapping (VSM) rather than focusing on the whole value stream. In the value stream, you look at a series of processes together. This gives better results and ensures the quality of improvement.

A focus on maximizing the efficiency and capability of a single process can negatively affect another process. It can create waste in another linked area. For example, one of the main lean goals is to make single-piece flow to improve the workflow and minimize the work-in-process inventory. If you assemble one piece of a product in ten minutes, wait to assemble ten pieces, and send them together in one large batch, that's one hundred minutes. Therefore, the time to assemble one piece has become one hundred minutes—even though the value-added time is only ten minutes. Moving one piece of a product every ten minutes will reduce the lead times of making the product, minimize the WIP inventory, and speed up the delivery to the customer. However, this will put more effort and strain on the transportation department—especially when the process steps are not close to each other. Therefore, improving the efficiency of the transportation process should also be considered with producing small batches.

Although analyzing the whole value stream usually yields good results over the analysis of the individual processes, analyzing the individual processes and improving them can give quicker results. When analyzing a series of processes in the value stream, there will usually be a series of linked issues. They will take a much longer time to be improved and might need to be divided into smaller issues. Each should go through the continuous improvement cycle. This will not usually work in companies that still don't believe in lean's workability. In such a culture, it is preferable to show quick results by looking at the processes that can be improved easily and quickly and avoiding waiting to improve the overall value stream. This can take a much longer time to fix. When top management sees quick results from lean, they will provide the support needed for more improvement.

VSM is a good lean tool. It is not exactly a tool for process improvement but a tool to ensure that process-improvement efforts do the following:

- Fit together from process to process so that a flowing value stream is developed.
- Match with the organization's targets and business needs.
- Serve the requirements of external customers.

Some companies utilize VSM to make random improvements for every piece of work, but they don't have clear visions based on current situations and real business needs. It is better to perform VSM based on reasonable objectives and specific plans in order to serve long-term business goals and improve the overall company's business process.

References

Ahmed, M.H. (2014). Daily Walks Train Future Leaders. Industrial Management 56 (1): 22–27.
Google Scholar[1]

Ahmed, M.H. (2013). Lean Transformation Guidance: Why Organizations Fail to Achieve and Sustain Excellence through Lean Improvement. International Journal of Lean Thinking 4 (1): 31–40.
Google Scholar[2]

Balle, M. and Balle, F. (2014) Lead with Respect: A Novel of Lean Practice, Lean Enterprise Institute, Cambridge.

Balle, M. and Balle, F. (2010) Lean Manager: A Novel of Lean Transformation. Lean Enterprise Institute, Cambridge.

Byrne, A. (2012) The Lean Turnaround: How Business Leaders Use Lean Principles to Create Value and Transform Their Company. McGraw-Hill, New York.

Drucker, P. F. (1954). The Practice of management. New York: HarperCollins Publishers.

Kaufman, J. (2012) The Personal MBA: Master the Art of Business, Portfolio Publishing, New York.

Taylor, F. W. (1911). The principles of scientific management. New York: Harper & Brothers.

Liker, J. K., & Convis, G. L. (2012). Toyota way to lean leadership: Achieving and sustaining excellence through leadership development. New York: MacGraw-hill.

Liker, J. K. (2002) The Toyota Way: 14 Management Principles from the World's Greatest Manufacturer, McGraw-Hill, New York.

---

1. https://scholar.google.com/
scholar_lookup?hl=en&volume=56&publication_year=2014&pages=22-27&issue=1&author=M.+H.+Ahmed&title=Daily+walks+train+future+leaders

2. http://scholar.google.com/
scholar_lookup?hl=en&volume=4&publication_year=2013&pages=31-40&issue=1&author=M.+H.+Ahmed&title=Lean+transformation+guidance%3A+Why+organizations+fail+to+achieve+and+sustain+excellence+through+lean+improvement

Liker, J.K. (2011). Toyota Under Fire: Lessons for Turning Crisis into Opportunity. McGraw-Hill, New York.

Rother, M. (2009). Toyota Kata: Managing People for Improvement, Adaptiveness, And Superior Results. New York: Macgraw-Hill.

Rick Harris, Chris Harris, Earl Wilson, Jim Womack, Dan Jones, John Shook, Jose Ferro. 2003. Making Materials Flow: A Lean Material-Handling Guide for Operations, Production-Control, and Engineering Professionals; version 1.0 Edition.

Rother, M., and R. Harris. 2001. Creating Continuous Flow: An Action Guide for Managers, Engineers and Production Associates. Cambridge, MA: Lean Enterprise Institute.

Roy F. Baumeister and Brad J. Bushman. 2020. Social psychology and human nature. Cengage Learning.

Liker, J. K. and Trachilis, G. (2015) Developing Lean Leaders at All Levels: A Practical Guide, Lean Leadership Institute Publications, Cambridge.

Liker, J. K., Convis, G. L. (2012). Toyota Way to Lean Leadership: Achieving and Sustaining Excellence through Leadership Development. New York: Macgraw-Hill.

Liker, J. K., Trachilis, G. (2015). Developing Lean Leaders at All Levels: A Practical Guide. Cambridge, MA: Lean Leadership Institute Publications.

Liker, J. K., Meier, D. (2005). Toyota Talent: Developing Your People the Toyota Way. New York: McGraw-Hill.

Liker, J. K., and K. J. Franz. 2011. The Toyota Way to Continuous Improvement: Linking Strategy and Operational Excellence to Achieve Superior Performance. New York: McGraw-Hill.

Rother, M. (2009). Toyota Kata: Managing People for Improvement, Adaptiveness, And Superior Results. New York: Macgraw-Hill.

Shook. J. (2008). Managing to Learn: Using the A3 Management Process to Solve Problems, Gain Agreement, Mentor and Lead. Cambridge, MA: Lean Enterprise Institute.

Soliman, M.H.A. (2016). Hoshin Kanri: How Toyota Creates a Culture of Continuous Improvement to Achieve Lean Goals. SC: CreateSpace.

Google Scholar[3]

Soliman, M.H.A. (2015). A New Routine for Culture Change. Industrial Management 57 (3): 25–30.

Google Scholar[4]

Soliman, M.H.A. (2015). What Toyota Production System Is Really About? Unpublished. https://www.researchgate.net/publication/280557330_What_Toyota_Production_System_is_Really_About

Soliman, M. H. A. (2020). The Toyota Way to Effective Strategy Deployment: How Organizations Can Focus Energy on Key Priorities Through Hoshin Kanri to Achieve the Business Goals. Journal of Operations and Strategic Planning 3(1), 1-27. Sage Publications. DOI: https://doi.org/10.1177/2516600X20946542

Google Scholar[5]

Soliman, M. H. A. (2017). Why Continuous Improvement Programs Fail in the Egyptian Manufacturing Organizations? A Research Study of the Evidence. AJIBM 7(3).

Google Scholar[6]

Soliman, M. H. A. (2017). A COMPREHENSIVE REVIEW OF MANUFACTURING WASTES: TOYOTA PRODUCTION SYSTEM LEAN PRINCIPLES. EJER 22(2), 1-10.

Google Scholar[7]

Soliman, M. H. A. 2020. Gemba Walks the Toyota Way: The Place to Teach and Learn Management. KDP.

ResearchGate[8]

Soliman, M. H. A. 2020. 5S: A Practical Guide to Visualizing and Organizing Workplaces to Improve Productivity.

ResearchGate[9]

---

3. https://scholar.google.com/scholar?hl=en&q=Soliman+M.+H.+A.+%282016%29.+Hoshin+Kanri%3A+How+Toyota+creates+a+culture+of+continuous+improvement+to+achieve+lean+goals.+CreateSpace.

4. https://scholar.google.com/scholar_lookup?hl=en&volume=57&publication_year=2015&pages=25-30&issue=3&author=M.+H.+A.+Soliman&title=A+new+routine+for+culture+change

5. https://scholar.google.com/scholar?oi=bibs&hl=en&cluster=17062018057766024444

6. https://scholar.google.com/scholar?oi=bibs&hl=en&cluster=8021810583850012517

7. https://scholar.google.com/scholar?oi=bibs&hl=en&cluster=11010695423475619303

8. https://www.researchgate.net/publication/345642377_Gemba_Walks_the_Toyota_Way_The_Place_to_Teach_and_Learn_Management

Soliman, M. H. A. 2020. Takt Time: A Guide to the Very Basic Lean Calculation. KDP.

ResearchGate[10]

Soliman, M. H. A. 2020. Kanban the Toyota Way: An Inventory Buffering System to Eliminate Inventory. KDP.

SSRN[11]

Soliman, M. H. A. 2015. Developing People Improves the Process. Industrial Management 58(1).

Google Scholar[12]

Soliman, M. H. A. 2020. Turning PDCA into a Routine for Learning. KDP.

Soliman, M. H. A. 2020. Lean Accounting: Why Accounting Department Should Switch to Lean. KDP.

Soliman, M. H. A. 2020. 5S: A Practical Guide to Visualizing and Organizing Workplaces to Improve Productivity. KDP.

Soliman, M. H. A. 2020. Jidoka: The Toyota Principle of Building Quality into the Process. KDP.

Soliman, M. H. A. 2018. Healthcare is Ripe for Lean. Industrial Management.

---

9. https://www.researchgate.net/publication/345393902_5S_A_Practical_Guide_to_Visualizing_and_Organizing_Workplaces_to_Improve_Productivity

10. https://www.researchgate.net/publication/345123642_Takt_Time_A_Guide_to_the_Very_Basic_Lean_Calculation

11. https://papers.ssrn.com/sol3/papers.cfm?abstract_id=3722480

12. https://scholar.google.com/scholar?oi=bibs&hl=en&cluster=467901078499471580

About the Author

Mohammed Hamed Ahmed Soliman is an industrial engineer, consultant, university lecturer, operational excellence leader, and author. He works as a lecturer at the American University in Cairo and as a consultant for several international industrial organizations.

Soliman earned a bachelor of science in Engineering and a master's degree in Quality Management. He earned post-graduate degrees in Industrial Engineering and Engineering Management. He holds numerous certificates in management, industry, quality, and cost engineering.

For most of his career, Soliman worked as a regular employee for various industrial sectors. This included crystal-glass making, fertilizers, and chemicals. He did this while educating people about the culture of continuous improvement.

Soliman has lectured at Princess Noura University and trained the maintenance team in Vale Oman Pelletizing Company. He has been lecturing at The American University in Cairo for 6 year and has designed and delivered 40 leadership and technical skills enhancement training modules.

Soliman is a member at the Institute of Industrial and Systems Engineers and a member with the Society for Engineering and Management Systems. He has published several articles in peer reviewed academic journals and magazines. His writings on lean manufacturing, leadership, productivity, and business appear in Industrial Engineers, Lean Thinking, and Industrial Management. Soliman's blog is www.personal-lean.org.

Don't miss out!

Visit the website below and you can sign up to receive emails whenever Mohammed Hamed Ahmed Soliman publishes a new book. There's no charge and no obligation.

https://books2read.com/r/B-A-VCQM-VZRCC

BOOKS2READ

Connecting independent readers to independent writers.

Also by Mohammed Hamed Ahmed Soliman

Hoshin Kanri: How Toyota Creates a Culture of Continuous Improvement to Achieve Lean Goals

Industrial Applications of Infrared Thermography: How Infrared Analysis Can be Used to Improve Equipment Inspection

Ultrasound Analysis for Condition Monitoring: Applications of Ultrasound Detection for Various Industrial Equipment

Brainstorming for Problems Solving: How Leaders Can Achieve a Successful Brainstorming Session

Lean Accounting : Why Accounting Department Should Switch to Lean

Turning PDCA into a Routine for Learning

5S: A Practical Guide to Visualizing and Organizing Workplaces to Improve Productivity

5S: A Practical Guide to Visualizing and Organizing Workplaces to Improve Productivity

Hoshin Kanri: How Toyota Creates a Culture of Continuous Improvement to Achieve Lean Goals

Industrial Applications of Infrared Thermography: How Infrared Analysis Can be Used to Improve Equipment Inspection

The Seven Deadly Wastes and How to Remove Them from Your Business: The Heart of the Toyota Production System

Ultrasound Analysis for Condition Monitoring: Applications of Ultrasound Detection for Various Industrial Equipment

Manufacturing Wastes Stream: Toyota Production System Lean Principles and Values

Takt Time: A Guide to the Very Basic Lean Calculation

Toyota Standard Work: The Foundation of Kaizen

Jidoka: The Toyota Principle of Building Quality into the Process

Machine Reliability and Condition Monitoring: A Comprehensive Guide to Predictive Maintenance Planning

Gemba Walks the Toyota Way : The Place to Teach and Learn Management

Overall Equipment Effectiveness Simplified: Analyzing OEE to find the Improvement Opportunities

Practical Guide to FMEA : A Proactive Approach to Failure Analysis

Toyota Healthcare: 7+1 Types Of Waste

The Ultimate Guide to Successful Lean Transformation: Top Reasons Why Companies Fail to Achieve and Sustain Excellence through Lean Improvement

Machinery Oil Analysis & Condition Monitoring : A Practical Guide to Sampling and Analyzing Oil to Improve Equipment Reliability

Kanban the Toyota Way: An Inventory Buffering System to Eliminate Inventory

Vibration Basics and Machine Reliability Simplified : A Practical Guide to Vibration Analysis

Risk Assessment Using FMEA: A Case of Reliable Improvement

The Problem Solving Kata as a Tool for Culture Change:
Building True Lean Organizations

Watch for more at https://www.personal-lean.org/.

About the Publisher

Personal-lean is dedicated to publish high quality educational content, assessment, training in the filed of business for various industrial sectors. And is a growing educational organization, with products and services in various countries.

www.ingramcontent.com/pod-product-compliance
Lightning Source LLC
Chambersburg PA
CBHW031542210526
45464CB00003B/1113